THE UNSPOILED WEST

THE UNSPOILED WEST

THE WESTERN LANDSCAPE AS SEEN BY ITS GREATEST PHOTOGRAPHERS

EDITED BY

JEROME PRESCOTT

SMITHMARK

This edition published in 1995
by SMITHMARK Publishers Inc.,
16 East 32nd Street,
New York, New York 10016.

SMITHMARK books are available for bulk purchase for sales promotion and premium use. For details write or telephone the Manager of Special Sales, SMITHMARK Publishers Inc., 16 East 32nd Street, New York, NY 10016. (212) 532-6600.

Produced by Brompton Books Corp.,
15 Sherwood Place,
Greenwich, CT 06830.

ISBN 0-8317-9058-X

Printed in China

10 9 8 7 6 5 4 3 2

Page 1: This Ansel Adams photograph of a saguaro cactus, *Carnegiea gigantea,* was taken in Saguaro National Monument as part of the National Park Service Mural Project in the early 1940s. This magnificent cactus lends its distinctive profile to the southwestern desert landscape. Its roots can locate underground rivers, keeping it green throughout the driest months of summer. Its white flowers and red fruit offer delightful color contrast in the desert as well as food for the animals who live in that fragile environment.

Page 2: The Grand Canyon, shaped by the mighty Colorado River, was a source of inspiration to Ansel Adams. Adams took this view in 1941 during his work for the National Park Service's commissioned Mural Project. The striations in the canyon walls and the dark shadows of the canyon depths were perfect subjects for the exaggerated interplay between light and dark that Adams brought to all his photos.

Facing page: George Alexander Grant took this photo of the Oregon Coast in December 1938 while he was working for the National Park Service. Formed by ocean wave erosion, natural bridges are prevalent along the West Coast of the United States.

PREFACE

There was a time—through most of the first half of the twentieth century and beyond—when people talked about the American West as having been 'won' or 'tamed.' The taming of the American West was seen as a kind of triumph or victory of humankind over a belligerent wilderness.

The settlement of the West had been a challenge and a struggle and many an American breathed easier at the dawn of the twentieth century. When the wilderness had been bound and bisected by railroads, highways and barbed wire fences that stretched as far as the eye could see, the children of those early Americans inherited this pride of accomplishment and took the taming of the West as indeed a victory for the good guys. A dozen or so years past the century's midpoint, however, the grandchildren of the pioneers grew nostalgic for a past they had never known. They began to celebrate the notion of a primordial land untouched by human hands. A generation of backpackers left the interstate highways and trackless suburbs to search for the unspoiled remnants of the wilderness their ancestors had 'tamed.'

With the close of the first century since the end of America's frontier, we look back with nostalgia to the excitement of a time when the West still murmured to the primeval forces of nature, to that time when the scream of the eagle and the rhythm of the waterfall had not yet been usurped by the clatter of manmade contrivances. This book is an album of photographs made in that era—which still survives in the remote corners of this land—when white men were still timid trespassers in an unspoiled American West.

INTRODUCTION

Practical photography entered the world of popular culture in 1839, conceived in France by Joseph Nicephore Niepce a dozen years before and mid-wived by Louis Jacques Daguerre. Photography was an amazing and almost magical process in which images more delicate than the finest painting could be affixed to metal—and later glass—plates through the use of light and chemicals in moments rather than after weeks of work with paints and brushes.

Photography—or the making of 'daguerreotypes' as it was then known—seems to have come to the United States via the inventor and telegrapher Samuel FB Morse, who met Daguerre in Paris in 1839. By 1844, Morse's friend Mathew Brady had established a commercial daguerreotype studio at Fulton and Broadway in New York City. Brady went on to become one of the biggest names in early portrait photography, photographing all the notable people of the day and making more than a good living making portraits and selling scenic photographs.

General John Fremont had taken a daguerreotypist with him on his 1842 expedition to the West, but he failed to make any successful pictures. It was one of Mathew Brady's young assistants—the son of Irish immigrants—named Timothy O'Sullivan who was destined to be one of the earliest and most important photographers of the American West.

By the time the Civil War broke out in 1861, O'Sullivan was a photographer in his own right, and like Mathew Brady and many of the other major photographers of the era, he set out to make a photographic record of the war. A number of photographs had been made on the battlefields of the Crimean War in 1855, but for all practical purposes, the American Civil War was the first war to be fully documented by photographers. Brady's images of the war—particularly those of President Abraham Lincoln and his officers—are among the most famous, but Timothy O'Sullivan's are among the most moving. O'Sullivan photographed the battle scenes from Manassass to Bull Run and is especially remembered for his images of Gettysburg, the war's pivotal battle.

After the war, O'Sullivan became part of the US Geological Exploration of the Fortieth Parallel, a reconnaissance of the West under the leadership of Clarence King at the behest of the War Department. The idea was to survey a wide swath of the American West—working west to east—from San Francisco to Salt Lake City.

The King Expedition, as it was known, embarked for the West Coast by ship in May 1867 and left San Francisco to tackle the wilderness two months later. Thus it was that Timothy O'Sullivan became the first professional photographer to systematically survey the American West. The King party crossed

Previous page: This photograph of Yellowstone Lake and Mt Sheridan was part of a series of images Ansel Adams was asked to assemble advocating conservation of the wilderness. Adams' photographs are more than instructional, they are images of hope and a call to action. In a letter to David McAlpin, Adams wrote: 'If I feel I have any niche at all in the photographic presentation of America, I think it would be chiefly to show the land and sky as the settings for human activity. And it would be showing also how man could be related to this magnificent setting, and how foolish it is that we have the disorganization and misery that we have.'

Facing page: William Henry Jackson used portable darkrooms such as the one pictured here to develop his prints. He took this view of the rocks below Platte Canyon in 1874 in Douglas County, Colorado.

the Sierra Nevada, passing the workmen of the Central Pacific Railroad who would complete their rail crossing of that rugged mountain range the following year. Dodging bands of often-hostile Indians, King and his men crossed the desolate, tarantula-infested, alkaline wastes of the Great Basin and passed the Great Salt Lake.

Through all of this, O'Sullivan continued to compile his photographic record, using a small horse-drawn ambulance wagon that he'd converted into a portable darkroom. Not only did he develop his huge glass plate negatives as he went, but he also *manufactured* them. The photographic technology of the 1860s required that the silver compound photographic emulsion be painted on the plates and the plates exposed while still wet. The mass production of 'dry plates' was to be invented by George Eastman of Rochester, New York, in 1879, by which time much of the American West had been documented by early photographers using wet plates.

King, O'Sullivan and their group surveyed the Sierra, the Great Basin and the Rockies for over a year, arriving in Salt Lake City in October 1868.

In 1871, after a survey of the Isthmus of Panama, O'Sullivan was attached to another US War Department survey of the West, this one under the leadership of Captain George Montague Wheeler of the US Army. By 1871, Wheeler, an 1866 graduate of West Point, was no stranger to the West. He'd served as engineering officer to the US Army's California Department and had surveyed most of the West from Idaho to Arizona. The 1871 Wheeler Expedition, which O'Sullivan documented, overlapped the King Survey in Nevada and Utah, but also extended its coverage into the deserts and mountains of Arizona and Southern California, including Death Valley.

During the expedition, Wheeler led his team on a 200-mile boat and barge trip up the Colorado River from California to the heart of the Grand Canyon in Arizona, in the course of which O'Sullivan barely escaped losing his equipment and plates when his boat was almost wrecked going over the thundering rapids. In this instance, disaster was averted. However, the expedition ultimately ended in tragedy. Many, if not most, of O'Sullivan's several hundred glass plate negatives disappeared mysteriously en route to San Francisco at the end of the expedition, and Fred Loring, a young Bostonian who had traveled with the party as a correspondent for *Appleton's Journal of Literature*, was killed when the stagecoach carrying him on the first leg of his return to the East was ambushed by Apaches.

Timothy O'Sullivan's surviving photographs made him a celebrity of sorts in both the East and the West. His pictures helped to give the people of the United States—then concentrated in the East—a sense of the profound scenic beauty of the wild land between the plains and California. His biographers can find no trace of what happened to O'Sullivan in 1874, but in 1875 he rejoined Wheeler for a last trip to the West that he had helped to immortalize. When he returned home from that expedition, he was named by his mentor, Clarence King, to serve as the first official photographer of the newly-established US Geologic Survey.

The US Geologic Survey was really the culmination of the efforts of many and was inspired by the expeditions undertaken by Clarence King and George Wheeler, as well as John Wesley Powell and Dr Ferdinand Vanderveer Hayden. Hayden was a medical doctor turned geologist who divided his time between his chair as a professor of geology at the University of Pennsylvania and his saddle, from which he surveyed much of the Mountain West between 1853 and 1879.

The US Geological & Geographical Survey of the Territories, which Hayden headed from 1869 to 1879, was the true precursor to the US Geologic Survey, with which he served from 1879 to 1886. The US Geological & Geographical Survey of the Territories was divided into two divisions, with Hayden himself leading Division One and John Wesley Powell leading Division Two.

It was through the efforts of Hayden and his staff that a unique 2.2 million-acre tract of land in Wyoming, Montana and Idaho became designated in 1872 as Yellowstone National Park. The idea of an unspoiled section of the West being set aside as 'free from any exploitation and for use of the people forever' was a revolutionary concept in an era when the West was perceived as being limitless and inexhaustible. Yellowstone was the first step in a national park system that now encompasses 68.2 million largely unspoiled acres—mostly in the West.

In his capacity as Geologist in Charge of the Geologic & Geographical Survey, it was Hayden's role to organize and lead field studies. To fill the important position of field photographer he chose young William Henry Jackson, a Vermont-born Civil War veteran who'd made a name for himself photographing the progress of the Union Pacific Railroad, which had met with the Central Pacific at Promontory, Utah on 10 May 1869 to form North America's first transcontinental railway link. With the nation now bound together by bands of steel, there was an

Above: In 1871, Lieutenant George Montague Wheeler was put in charge of a fourth Western survey, this time going south of the Central Pacific Railroad into eastern Nevada and Arizona. Wheeler chose Timothy O'Sullivan as the team photographer and Frederick W Loring, a young Bostonian writer from a wealthy family, to publicize the achievements of the expedition. O'Sullivan took this portrait of Fred Loring and his mule, Evil Merodach, in 1871. Loring's contempt for the native peoples he encountered was reflected in his articles for *Appleton's Journal of Literature*, which enraged the editors of local Pacific Coast papers. Local editors denounced Loring as a 'flop.' Ironically, Loring was killed by an Apache raiding party while enroute to the East at the end of the Wheeler expedition.

Right: The US Geological and Geographical Survey of the Territories was led by Ferdinand V Hayden, pictured here in front with the entire company on the trail between the Yellowstone and East Fork rivers in Wyoming Territory. The pack train was the way survey parties traveled in the wilderness. William Henry Jackson, who served as the expedition photographer, took this photograph in Yellowstone National Park in 1871.

enhanced interest in the vast territories to the north and south of the thin line of the railroad.

Back in Vermont, in the early part of 1866, Jackson had been the artist in a photographer's gallery at $25 a week. A year and a half later he relocated to Omaha, Nebraska, and worked for a photographer named Hamilton. In the late fall of 1867, convinced that he could make a go of it, he bought out Hamilton, with a token down payment. About the time he was concluding negotiations with Hamilton, his father offered to put up the rest of the money plus a small amount of operating capital if he would take his brother Ed in with him. By the middle of 1868 the firm of Jackson Brothers was in operation.

Omaha was a fine location for business. The town was old, as age is reckoned beyond the Mississippi—the first house was built in 1853—and it had at the same time the enormous vitality of a boom town. Omaha was the central marketplace for a prosperous farming country, and the Union Pacific Railroad operations had brought in many workers and traders. By the time Jackson Brothers arrived, Omaha was the unrivaled metropolis west of Chicago and north of St Louis.

But the factor that put William Henry Jackson on the map was the railroad. 'Here was something truly earth-shaking,' he recalled, 'and, whether or not there had been a dime in it for me, sooner or later I would have been out on the grade with my cameras.'

It is almost impossible to exaggerate the contemporary influence of the first transcontinental railway. Authorized by Congress in the midst of the Civil War, its real progress began only after Appomattox. The tempo increased from 1866 to 1867, and construction reached a dizzy climax during the summer of 1868, with the Central Pacific pushing from the west and the Union Pacific from the east. During the last months, the rival directors called a truce and agreed upon Promontory, Utah, as the meeting place for their respective lines. But in the popular mind the race continued, and people came from all over to watch the work. During the final weeks of construction the country about Ogden took on the aspects of a playground. Everybody who was anybody seemed to be hurrying west for the joining of the rails.

Though he'd made a name for himself photographing the progress of the Union Pacific Railroad, William Henry Jackson was not present at Promontory on 10 May 1869. One reason was that his business just wasn't big enough to support an expensive junket. Another had to do with Miss Mary Greer of Warren, Ohio, who had chosen that date to marry him. As Jackson wrote later, 'The joining of the rails became for the moment insignificant.'

Later in the summer, however, Jackson did go west again. He photographed the settlements of Wasatch, Blue Creek, Corinne, and Uintah, with many points of scenic interest that he was conveniently able to reach along the Union Pacific line. This was the period when he really developed his craft. The art of timing exposures was still so uncertain that one prayed every time the lens was uncapped, and no picture was a safe bet until the plate had been developed. Working in a fully equipped studio was hazardous enough. In the open of a field location, it involved, to quote Jackson, 'labor, patience and the moral stamina—or, perhaps, sheer phlegmatism—to keep on day after day, in spite of the overexposed and underdeveloped negatives, and without regard to the accidents to cameras and chemicals.'

Photography was still, of course, in the wet-plate stage, and for this trip he had contrived a portable dark room. It was a wooden box 30″ x 15″ x 15″ (762mm x 381mm x 381mm) fitted with pans and trays, and made so that it could be enlarged with a retractable canopy. This case was cumbersome enough to lug around; but it was extremely compact in comparison with the buggy studio that he'd used a year before. Jackson carried two cameras. The first was a standard 8″ x 10″ (203mm x 254mm).

The other was a stereo camera with a pair of brass-barreled Willard lenses that looked like 'a young cannon.' In addition to the bulky plates, he had a mass of chemicals, silver baths and developers. 'We may have looked as if we were ready for a picnic' Jackson wrote, 'but it wasn't one.'

Late in July 1869, he arrived in Salt Lake City with enough exposed negatives to pay for a dozen boxes of chemicals, but he couldn't turn the prints into cash because he lacked the materials to do the printing. Finally he borrowed the money from a baggage-master named McCoy at the Union Pacific, whom he had known in Omaha.

In eastern Utah he photographed the Golden Spike site at Promontory. Although a stretch of empty rail was in itself a dull subject, this particular section had established itself as a popular choice. He made expeditions to all the striking natural views of the surrounding country, such as Devil's Slide, Pulpit Rock, Death Rock, Monument Rock, Hanging Rock, Castle Rocks and Needle Rocks.

It was in Wyoming during that summer that Jackson had first met Dr Ferdinand Hayden. A graduate of Oberlin and a doctor of medicine, Hayden had never practiced his profession (except as a Union Army surgeon). Instead, he had elected to be a geologist. As early as 1853 he had gone into the West, and until his death in 1887 he never rested from his efforts to inform others about the unspoiled West. While some of the American Indians who encountered him regarded the geologist as insane, they were awed by Hayden's industry, and they named him Man-Who-Picks-Up-Stones-Running. Immediately after the war Hayden had become a professor of geology at the University of Pennsylvania. With his summers free for field work, he was also able to lead annual government parties to explore and survey the vast unmapped regions of the West.

On 23 July, 1870, on his way to Wyoming, Hayden called at Jackson's place of business in Omaha. He spent a long time studying Jackson's Union Pacific pictures and the Indian groups Jackson had photographed near Omaha. Finally, with a sigh, he remarked, 'This is what I need. I wish I could offer you enough to make it worth your while to spend the summer with me.'

'What could you offer?' Jackson asked quickly.

Hayden smiled. 'Only a summer of hard work—and the satisfaction I think you would find in contributing your art to science. Of course, all your expenses would be paid, but...'

Two days later Jackson agreed to join Hayden at Cheyenne 'as soon as possible.' Quickly he straightened out the affairs of his shop and left his wife in charge. With Hayden, Jackson, a half dozen scientists, the eight teamsters and helpers, there were 20 men on the 1870 Hayden expedition.

Jackson's equipment, plus extras and refinements, was the same he had carried the previous summer: the double-barreled stereo, and the 6.5″ x 8.5″ (164mm x 215mm) camera (also adaptable to stereoscopic work), the portable dark room, completely rebuilt and improved, a full stock of chemicals and enough glass for 400 plates. The whole must have weighed not less than 300 pounds. Since he had one of the two wheeled vehicles at his disposal, neither weight nor bulk mattered much. He also had Hypo, a fat little mule with cropped ears, who was almost as indispensable to Jackson as his namesake, hyposulfite of soda, was to darkroom chemistry.

Carrying Jackson's cameras, tripod, dark box, chemicals, water keg and a day's supply of plates, all loaded in big, brightly painted rawhide containers, Hypo was good for as many miles as Jackson's saddle horse was, and together they covered an enormous amount of ground off the road from the wagon party.

Following the Oregon-Mormon Trail as far as Fort Bridger, they then went into the Uinta Mountains for nearly three weeks and returned by way of the old Overland Trail. Next, Jackson and several of the party went to photograph the Pikes Peak region of Colorado.

The following year, on 10 June 1871, the second annual Hayden Survey broke camp in Ogden. The party numbered 34, as compared to 20 in 1870. The increase in personnel had been made possible through a larger Congressional appropriation, and in part the $40,000 put up in 1871 was a recognition of Dr Hayden's earlier work. However, the real interest in Washington lay not so much in what the Survey had already accomplished as in what it might find in the fabled Yellowstone country of northwestern Wyoming.

John Colter, a member of the Lewis and Clark Expedition, had probably been the first white man ever to set foot within the vast area now designated as Yellowstone National Park. When he came back to civilization after a solitary tour of the region in 1807, no one believed his tales of grottoes and geysers, tumbling cataracts and boiling sulphur fountains. It was not until 1852 that the slightest credence was placed in the Yellowstone legend. Furthermore, it was not until 1870 that the first fully organized and publicized expedition—under Henry D Washburn and NP

Langford—made its way into Yellowstone country. However, no photographs had as yet been published, and Hayden was determined that the first ones should be good. They would not only supplement his final report but tell the story to thousands who might never read it.

Jackson's equipment was substantially the same as he had used during the previous two seasons. This included an 8″ x 10″ (203mm x 254mm), a 6.5″ x 8.5″ (164mm x 215mm) and a stereoscopic camera. By this time he had rigged up his first gadget for 'speed' work—a drop shutter, actuated by a rubber band, that enabled him to shoot action at high noon with a one-tenth second exposure. However, most of his pictures were made with exposure times of five seconds or more. When speed was no consideration he always stopped his lens down to get maximum depth and definition.

Hayden, Jackson and their party entered Yellowstone from the north, which was then considered to be the easiest route. They had their first close view of the enchanted land when the party came upon the Mammoth Hot Springs.

With this subject matter close at hand, so rich and abundant, it was necessary for Jackson to move his dark box only several times. His invariable practice was to keep it in the shade, then, after carefully focusing his camera, to return to the box, sensitize a plate, hurry back to the camera while it was still moist, slip the plate into position and make the exposure. The next step was to return to the dark box and immediately develop the plate. He would then go through the entire process once more from a new position. Under average conditions a 'round trip' might take 45 minutes. At Mammoth Springs, however, there was so little shifting to do that he was able to cut the average time to less than 15 minutes. Another thing that helped was the hot water at his fingertips. By washing the plates in water that spilled from the springs at 160° Fahrenheit, he was able to cut the drying time by more than half.

The party next traveled up the Yellowstone to Tower Creek. At the point where that stream drops into the gorge the view is magnificent, but recording it on a glass plate from the bed beneath turned out to be Jackson's biggest photographic problem of the year. Clambering down, and even up, the steep sides of the canyon was a difficult task, as was moving the camera over the same precipitous route.

Ultimately, Jackson set up his camera at the bottom of the gorge. He would prepare a plate, back the holder with wet blotting paper, then slip and slide and tumble down to his

Above: John Hillers took this photo of survey team member Almon Harris Thompson near Kanab, Utah, in 1872 or 1873.

Right: John Wesley Powell led Division Two of the US Geological and Geographical Survey of the Territories. EO Beaman was the official photographer of the expedition from 1871 to 1872. This Beaman photo shows the first camp of the Powell Expedition on the Green River in Wyoming Territory.

camera and make the exposure. After taking the picture, he had to climb to the top carrying the exposed plate wrapped up in a moist towel. He succeeded in repeating the procedure four times and not a single plate had dried out before being developed.

Pictorially the climax of the expedition came with their week's stay at Yellowstone Falls and the Grand Canyon of the Yellowstone.

Photographs were essential to the fulfillment of Hayden's plan for publicizing this Survey, but his basic purpose was always exploration. Nevertheless, it was Jackson's photography that constituted the tangible results. They were the exhibits that

people saw and the exhibits considered when, without a dissenting vote, Congress established Yellowstone as the first national park, to be forever set aside for the people. On 1 March 1872, with the signature of President Grant, the bill became law.

Congress also made a liberal appropriation for another Hayden expedition, to explore Yellowstone Park more fully and to take in the Teton Range south of it. Jackson now added to his other equipment an 11" x 14" (279mm x 356mm) camera. The demand, as well as real need, for big pictures compelled that course, since satisfactory enlargements from smaller negatives could not be made. In the modern era of 35mm negatives, it is hard to think of his 8″ x 10″ (203mm x 254mm) or 6.5″ x 8.5″ (164mm x 215mm) negatives as 'small.'

Since it was impossible to prepare and develop the larger plates in his *portable* dark box, Jackson now had to set up a dark *tent* every time he wanted to make a picture.

A permanent camp was set up in the upper end of Teton Basin, then still a favored shelter for trappers. Jackson set out with his primary objective being the high tableland between the branches of the Teton River. Reaching the main plateau, at an altitude of about 11,000 feet (3,350 meters), he quickly set up his cameras and began one of the busiest picture-making days of his career. It was one of those rare days when everything he wanted could be photographed with hardly a shift of the dark tent.

Everything, that is, except water. His assistants filled their rubber water bags from a trickling snow bank, as Jackson crept under the small tent to coat a plate. When he pulled aside the flap a little later he looked up and saw upon a rock ledge not twenty feet beyond him a mountain sheep in dignified contemplation of the strange scene before him—a bewhiskered man under an absurd covering of orange-hued canvas. Jackson later mused that with a high-speed 35mm camera he might have snapped a dozen exposures, but as it was he couldn't take a single photograph of the ram before he darted away.

The Hayden Survey went into the field much earlier in 1873 than in any of the previous three years. When Jackson arrived in Denver on 14 May, he found the main camp already established on Clear Creek, two or three miles out of town, with James T Gardner in temporary charge of the expedition. On 30 May, Jackson set up his camera on Prospect Mountain for a close-up view of Long's Peak and started what he called 'the season's harvest.' For a month he photographed the Rocky Mountains, following the route indicated to him by Gardner.

The overcast weather in the Rockies presented some problems for Jackson. Today a clear sky, bright sun, still air and clouds to punctuate the background are always desirable, but in the 1870s clear, bright weather was essential. Photographers of that era had no fast emulsions to counteract the effects of overcast skies, or to 'stop' wind-driven foliage. They had no filters to define clouds and horizons against the sky. If the weather was good, Jackson could take as fine a picture as can be made today, but on bad days a great deal of patient manipulation of the chemicals was needed to produce acceptable negatives. Jackson also lost a number of glass negatives when a pack mule stampeded, but he was able to reshoot many of the views.

During 1874, the Survey made the trip to Mesa Verde in southern Colorado. On 9 September, the expedition found itself deep in Mancos Canyon, facing a flat, vertical wall rising some 200 feet (61 meters) above the ledge on which they were standing. Fifty feet (15 meters) above their heads, in a shallow cave, were the legendary prehistoric ruins of the apartment dwellings where the Anasazi and their descendants lived for over 700 years. It was then that William Henry Jackson became the first photographer to set up his camera within the largest prehistoric city in North America. Before Hayden had glanced at half a dozen of these incredible photographs, Jackson's work for the following season was determined in his mind. Jackson was to go back to Mesa Verde, take many more pictures and explore further. Hayden was a dynamic, intense man, yet never had Jackson seen him at such a high pitch of enthusiasm.

Jackson's 5″ x 8″ (126mm x 203mm) camera had proved so satisfactory the year before that he decided to rely upon it again, for both single and stereographic views. He wanted to have a large camera for certain pictures, and he picked a Scovill 20″ x 24″ (508mm x 610mm), that is, one taking a plate of 480 square inches—exactly twelve times the area of his 1874 negatives. Although he used it only for exceptional shots, Jackson found the big camera to be worth all the extra work that it required.

After revisiting Mesa Verde, Jackson went on to Arizona and New Mexico. On 12 August his party arrived at the Pueblo of Tewa. There they spent several days with the people who live there. In 1877, Jackson went back to the Southwest, to Santa Fe and the Moqui pueblos.

There was no shortage of subjects, but the photographs were a total failure. Dry film was beginning to come in to general use so Jackson decided to depend upon it and to leave all the usual chemicals and paraphernalia at home. From L Wamerke, a well-known London photographic supplier, he ordered a supply of 'sensitive negative tissues supplied in bands.' With his 8″ x 10″ (203mm x 254mm) camera and all the film, he could have carried the entire load on his back. However, in spite of using great care in handling the film, always changing the rolls in total darkness, packing the exposed film in tight, waterproof cans, with the dry climate of the region as an additional safeguard, there was no trace of an image when he developed the rolls in his own laboratory in Washington, DC!

Jackson attributed the problem to too long an interval between exposure and development. Even now, film deteriorates with time, and in 1877 the science of preparing light-

Above: William Henry Jackson *(left)* and CR Campbell *(right)* photographing atop the broken sedimentary layers of rock in the Tetons. The central peaks of the Teton Range stand in the distance. This image was developed in 1872 in Lincoln County, Wyoming.

Right: This photograph of Mukuntuweap Valley in Zion Canyon, Utah, was taken in April 1872 by James Fennemore who apprenticed John K Hillers during the Powell Survey of southern Utah. Hillers is the figure reclining on the ledge.

Denver, Colorado and Detroit, Michigan. One of Jackson's assistants at his Detroit studio, Henry Peabody, went on to become a major Western photographer in his own right. Jackson died at the age of 99 in 1942, but spent his last years traveling by automobile through the West that he had first photographed 70 years before.

An important contemporary of William Henry Jackson was John Karl 'Jack' Hillers. His chance meeting with Major John Wesley Powell in May 1871 paralleled that between Jackson and Ferdinand Hayden two years before. Like Jackson he'd been an enlistee in the Union Army during the Civil War, and like Jackson he'd made a trip to California before taking up photography.

John Wesley Powell, like Clarence King, George Wheeler and Hayden before him, was an individualist who merged his lust for adventure with a firm dedication to the idea of surveying the West and documenting his observations. He enlisted in the Union Army in 1861. Despite the loss of his right arm in the Battle of Shiloh, Powell served to the end of the war and was discharged a major. He became a professor of natural history at Illinois Normal University and led two expeditions to the West in 1867 and 1868, exploring the upper Colorado River country.

In 1871, Powell was commissioned by Congress to undertake a more detailed expedition into the West as Division Two of the US Geological & Geographical Survey of the Territories. In 1871 his path crossed that of Jack Hillers, who happened to be in Salt Lake City, and who was hired as a boatman for the Colorado River trip. With an interest in photography, Hillers wound up as an assistant to EO Beaman, the expedition's official photographer. Beaman left the Powell Survey in January 1872, and Hillers, who'd shown both interest and skill, was selected to join Clem Powell and James Fennemore as an official photographer for Powell's March-September 1872 foray into the Grand Canyon and the surrounding plateau country. In October, Hillers went on to photograph the native peoples of the Hopi pueblos.

The equipment used by Hillers was essentially the same as that used by other early photographers. Most of his memorable work was done with an 11″ x 14″ (279mm x 356mm) view camera, although he also used 8″ x 10″ (203mm x 254mm) and 5″ x 8″ (126mm x 203mm) format cameras.

In April 1873 Hillers photographed the Grand Canyon, as well as many of the other Colorado and tributary canyons such as the Parunuweap, the Virgin and Zion. He also went into the Green River country of Wyoming.

sensitive emulsions was inexact. The disaster of that summer would haunt Jackson for the rest of his life.

In 1878, Hayden and Jackson returned to Montana and Wyoming. Since the ascent into the Wind River Mountains was impossible for pack mules, Jackson couldn't carry cumbersome wet-plate equipment. He decided that it was a case of dry plates or nothing, and so, since he had nothing to lose, Jackson decided to try a colloidobromide dry emulsion. It was slow, but otherwise dependable. In camp the night before the final climb he coated some plates and dried them over a shovel. Then, with nightmares of New Mexico and Arizona and the blank film of 1877, he slept.

The next day he found perfect working conditions on Fremont Peak, and in the evening he developed his negatives. They were good (even if one or two bore slight marks of the shovel). The important thing to Jackson was not so much the quality as his knowledge that he had finally found a satisfactory dry film.

Jackson left the Hayden Survey in 1878 and eventually worked for many years as a professional photographer in

Hillers spent early 1875 photographing the people on the Indian reservations in Oklahoma Territory and Indian Territory and went back to Utah in July. Returning to Washington, DC, in the fall of 1875, Hillers spent the winter preparing photographs of the unspoiled West for display at the US Centennial Exposition that would be held in Philadelphia in the summer of 1876.

In 1879, the Hayden, King, Powell and Wheeler Geological & Geographical surveys were merged into the new United States Geographical Survey, headed by Clarence King. John Wesley Powell transferred to the Smithsonian Institution to head a Bureau of Ethnology dedicated to the study of the soon-to-fade cultures of America's native peoples. He returned to the West, taking Hillers with him as the official photographer. It was the same drill as in the early 1870s, except that they now answered to a different agency—although Powell managed to have Hillers paid by the Geologic Survey.

Hillers went back into Arizona and New Mexico, conducting a detailed photographic study of the people of the pueblos in the upper Rio Grande Valley between 1879 and 1882.

In 1883, at age 40, Hillers married Elizabeth Schierenbeck and settled in Washington, DC, where he worked at printing and organizing photographs for both the Geological Survey and Powell's Bureau of Ethnology. He returned to the Southwest in 1885 and visited Yosemite Valley in 1892, but for the most part, his work in the West was behind him. He died in 1925.

By the dawn of the twentieth century, as the era of the 'wild' West was drawing to a close, many photographers had gone west to capture the last rays of afternoon light on a fading era. They came west facing many of the physical hardships faced by O'Sullivan, Jackson and Hillers, but they came blessed with the practical dry plate technology introduced by George Eastman in 1879, which made photography far easier than it had been before. Thomas McKee set up shop in Montrose, Colorado and documented the Ute Indians and the artifacts of their long-absent precursors. He conducted a thorough survey of Mesa Verde with his 11″ x 14″ (279mm x 356mm), 5″ x 7″ (126mm x 177mm) and stereoscopic cameras in 1900.

Frank Nowell reached Alaska as a young man in 1886, when most of that rugged territory and Canada's adjacent Yukon Territory were still not only unspoiled, but unexplored, except by the native Inuit and Tlingit people.

Shortly after the turn of the century, Edward S Curtis came on the scene as perhaps the most memorable photographer of

Left: Much of the exploration of the canyons and tributaries in Utah required travel by boat. From left to right: WD Johnson, Jr, FS Dellenbaugh and Jack Hillers are caulking the *Canonita* at the mouth of the Dirty Devil River in Utah, on 23 June 1872.

North America's native peoples. His work took him from Alaska to Montana to the Southwest.

Perhaps the most renowned photographer of the pristine American West in the middle twentieth century was Ansel Adams. Born in San Francisco in 1902, he was a son of the West. Adams grew up within sight of the rugged Pacific coastline which was literally the westernmost of the West and which was for the most part still unmarred by human hands while he was growing up there. Adams was introduced to photography as a child by his father, who was an accomplished amateur, but the spark that ignited his interest in becoming a landscape photographer was a 1916 family outing to Yosemite National Park. He was taken with its natural beauty, and in 1920, at the age of 18, he took a job as the custodian of the Sierra Club's headquarters in Yosemite.

Ansel Adams shot many early photographs of Yosemite and the Pacific coast with a Kodak Brownie camera, but as his interest in photography grew, so did the format size of his

Despite the fact that Eadweard Muybridge had photographed Yosemite as early as the 1860s, Adams will always be remembered as Yosemite's greatest photographer.

Though he remained rooted in Yosemite and Northern California, Adams photographed the Canadian Rockies in 1928 and made an extended trip to the Southwest, visiting the Grand Canyon, the pueblos of the Rio Grande Valley and eventually Santa Fe the following year.

In 1941, Harold Ickes, Secretary of the US Department of the Interior, commissioned Ansel Adams to produce a series of photographs of the national parks and monuments to be used in a series of murals in the Department of Interior headquarters in Washington, DC. Beginning in October 1941, Adams photographed Zion, the Grand Canyon, Canyon de Chelly and Carlsbad Caverns in the Southwest. The following June, he went on to photograph Rocky Mountain National Park in Colorado, Yellowstone and Grand Teton in Wyoming and Glacier in northern Montana.

While in Yellowstone, he sent greetings to William Henry Jackson, who had been the first to photograph the wonders of Yellowstone almost seven decades before. A few months later, Jackson died in New York City at the age of 99. It was as though a circle had been completed.

The Department of Interior Mural Project was terminated in July 1942, but in 1946 and 1948, Adams took up the project on his own. This took him to the parks encompassing Mt McKinley and Glacier Bay in Alaska and to Mt Rainier and the Olympic Peninsula in Washington.

He would spend the next four decades dividing his time between his beloved Yosemite and the Pacific coast, earning a reputation as perhaps the twentieth century's greatest interpreter of the unspoiled West. He would inspire at least two generations of photographers who still walk the wilderness in his footsteps. Ansel Adams died in 1984, bringing to a close his unique chapter in the photographic history of the unspoiled West.

Today the smog hangs low in Yosemite Valley and traffic clogs the roads of Yellowstone. Thousands of visitors stream to the rims of the Grand Canyon and television commercials are filmed in Monument Valley. That part of the West which remains unspoiled shrinks every year, but through the pioneering efforts of these great photographers, the magic of a pristine wilderness speaks to us across the decades and lives on in images captured on wet emulsions and plate glass negatives so long ago.

Above: This photograph of Jack Hillers on the Aquarius Plateau in southern Utah was taken either by Almon Harris Thompson or Grove Karl Gilbert, in July 1875, shortly before Hillers returned to Washington, DC, to prepare his photographs for the United States' centennial celebration in Philadelphia. In his hands is a large glass plate negative. His camera is in the center of the frame.

photographic equipment. In 1923, he acquired a Korona 6.5" x 8.5" (164mm x 215mm) view camera. The quality of his work improved immensely with the Korona, but it was not until 1927 that he felt that he had, as he described it, achieved 'the expression of my visualization through my technique—aesthetic, intellectual and mechanical.' Adams had used a Wratten 29 red filter to resolve an image of Half Dome in Yosemite, revealing the 'expressive-emotional quality' of the scene. With this image, Adams felt that he had achieved his 'first true visualization!'

As he recalled, 'I had been able to realize a desired image: not the way the subject appeared in reality but how it *felt* to me and how it must appear in the finished print. The sky had actually been a light, slightly hazy blue and the sunlit areas of Half Dome were moderately dark gray in value. The red filter dramatically darkened the sky and the shadows on the great cliff. Luckily I had with me the filter that made my visualized image possible.' With this event, our view of the unspoiled American West gained one of its greatest interpreters.

PLATE 1

Timothy O'Sullivan
Shoshone Falls on the Snake River

In 1868, Timothy O'Sullivan explored the canyons around the Snake River in southern Idaho. He captured this image near Shoshone Falls where the King Expedition had set up camp.

PLATE 2

Timothy O'Sullivan
Surveying in Shoshone Canyon

A member of the Clarence King Geological Exploration of the 40th Parallel is surveying from a rock near their camp in Shoshone Canyon above the falls.

PLATE 3

Timothy O'Sullivan
The Mouth of Paria Creek

Timothy O'Sullivan was the first photographer to make a systematic survey of the American West. He took this view looking across the mighty Colorado River to the mouth of Paria Creek in 1871.

PLATE 4

Timothy O'Sullivan
View on Shoshone Falls

Timothy O'Sullivan spent 1866 to 1869 in an area bordered by the Sierra Nevada, Washee and Wasatch Mountains. The water's glassy appearance in this view from the top is probably due to the long-exposure.

PLATE 5

William Henry Jackson
Crater of the Castle Geyser

William Henry Jackson photographed the crater of Castle Geyser in 1871. The beautiful hot spring in the center is nearly circular and funnel-shaped. The water is clear turquoise blue and has a constant temperature of 172° (78°C).

PLATE 6

William Henry Jackson
Black Sand Spring

Jackson, in an area that would become the world's first protected wilderness park, made this photograph at the Upper Firehole in Yellowstone in 1871.

407. BLACK SAND SPRING, UPPER FIRE HOLE.

PLATE 7

William Henry Jackson
Lower Yellowstone Falls

From atop Artist Point in 1871, William Henry Jackson captured the hidden splendor of Yellowstone.

PLATE 8

William Henry Jackson
Close-up of the Lower Yellowstone Falls

Plunging 308 feet (94 meters), the magnificent Lower Yellowstone Falls is nearly twice as tall as Niagara Falls. This close-up of the thunderous cascade is one of the park's breathtaking sights.

PLATE 9

William Henry Jackson
Grand Canyon of the Yellowstone

This Jackson photograph was taken in 1871 from the east bank of the Grand Canyon of the Yellowstone. The canyon is visible only from overlooks in this area.

PLATE 10

William Henry Jackson
Yellowstone River Above the Falls

Jackson photographed this narrow, rock-bound channel just above the Upper Falls on the Yellowstone in 1871.

YELLOWSTONE RIVER ABOVE THE FALLS.

PLATE 11

William Henry Jackson
Little Firehole Falls

Yellowstone would become a national park in 1872, one year after Jackson photographed the amazing terrain explored by the Hayden expedition. Little Firehole Falls, a multi-tiered hot waterfall, made a good subject for Jackson's camera.

PLATE 12

Timothy O'Sullivan
Sand Dunes in Carson Desert

From the redwoods on the West Coast to the sand dunes in the Carson Desert, Timothy O'Sullivan photographed the unspoiled West in all its diversity.

Both the Wheeler and the King surveys passed through the Carson Desert in Nevada. This view of a field of sand dunes gives one a sense of the isolation that O'Sullivan must have experienced on his solo expeditions. The vast emptiness of the desert and the tons of sand reflecting the sun's rays was a picture that would make settlers think twice before making the trek west over the Oregon Trail.

PLATE 13

Timothy O'Sullivan
Oak Grove, Sierra Blanca Range,
Arizona

O'Sullivan employed the same photographic technique in the American Southwest as he did when he photographed Civil War battlefields. He chose a perspective that placed the viewer in the scene by positioning his camera at eye-level.

This 1873 photo of an oak tree is a good example of how a simple image can symbolize an entire concept. A solitary man walking toward the shade of an oak tree gives one the impression of an unspoiled and hospitable landscape.

PLATE 14

William Henry Jackson
The Grand Teton

This towering peak was originally named Mount Hayden. In 1872, William Henry Jackson photographed Grand Teton and the area that would become Grand Teton National Park.

PLATE 15

Timothy O'Sullivan
The Colorado River

O'Sullivan took this view of the Colorado River from the rim of the Grand Canyon near the Devil's Anvil in 1871.

PLATE 16

William Henry Jackson
Sandbank

This photograph of a lone figure on a sandbank was taken circa 1873. Canyons continue to be shaped by the rivers which flow through them.

PLATE 17

William Henry Jackson
Tower Creek Falls From Above

This 1871 view looking down on Tower Creek Falls from above required climbing expertise as well as photographic skill. Jackson had to transport his camera up the steep trail 132 feet (40 meters) to the top of Tower Falls.

PLATE 18

William Henry Jackson
Tower Creek Falls From Below

Tower Falls was named for the adjacent volcanic pinnacles. In this view from below the falls, a tiny figure is visible on the boulder at the top of the stream. The photographs taken by William Henry Jackson of Tower Falls were among the more challenging to achieve technically.

GRAND CANYON. COLORADO RIVER LOOKING WEST.

PLATE 19

James Fennemore
View of Grand Canyon from Lava

Fennemore took this photograph of the inner gorge of the Grand Canyon looking west along the Colorado River in April 1872 as part of the Powell Survey. The figure visible on the top ledge overlooking the canyon is John K Hillers. Hillers assisted Fennemore in photographing the North Rim of the Grand Canyon.

PLATE 20

John Hillers and James Fennemore
Lava Falls Rapids in Grand Canyon

This photograph was taken on 19 or 20 April 1872. Fennemore and Hillers tried to capture the swirl and roar of the powerful rapids. This photograph is made possible by the slow exposure time demanded by the equipment.

John Hillers and James Fennemore
Side Canyon in Glen Canyon

The Powell Survey of 1872 explored many canyons and rivers in the West. In the Four Corners area, the point where the corners of four states meet—Colorado, Utah, New Mexico and Arizona—John Hillers and James Fennemore took some of their best photos. This view of a side canyon in Glen Canyon along the Colorado River in Utah was taken 2 July 1872.

The Colorado River flows south through Cataract Canyon, known for its 14-miles (23 km) of treacherous rapids, into Glen Canyon where it forms Lake Powell. The river then flows into Marble Canyon in Arizona and on to the Grand Canyon, into Nevada's Lake Mead, past the Hoover Dam, along California's state line and into Mexico where the mouth of the Colorado River empties into the Gulf of California.

PLATE 22

John Hillers
Marble Canyon

This photograph was taken on 22 August 1872, looking upriver and showing the canyon above the mouth of Nankoweap Canyon. At this point in the expedition, Hillers was no longer an assistant to the photographer, but a photographer in his own right.

41

PLATE 23

John Hillers
*Repairing Boats At the Foot of
Granite Rapid, Grand Canyon*

This Powell survey team had survived
the arduous pass through the hostile
rapids in Granite Canyon. The boats
were badly in need of repair and Hillers
took this photograph on 1 September
1872. FS Dellenbaugh is on the left.
Dana Butte (5034 feet/1534 meters tall)
is in the center distance. By 7 September,
the team reached the mouth of Kanab
Canyon.

PLATE 24

John Hillers
Field of Prickly Pear (Opuntia)
Cactus, Kanab Canyon, Arizona

After the difficult river trip through Granite Canyon, Hillers and Clem Powell remained in Kanab Canyon to take photographs. Among those Hillers took on 15 September 1872 was this field of prickly pear cactus. Hillers noted, 'Lots of cactus apples grow all along the side of the canyon—eat lots of them every day. They are a delicious fruit and I think very healthy.'

MARBLE PINNACLE KANAB CAN

PLATE 25

John Hillers
Marble Pinnacle, Kanab Canyon,
Arizona

Hillers took this photograph on 15
September 1872. Hillers wrote, 'The
canyon often doubles on itself, leaving
only a thin wall in the bend. Photographed one today measuring in height
over 2000 feet (600 meters), all marble,
measuring through its base only about
200 feet (60 meters).'

PLATE 26

John Hillers
Reflected Tower, Rio Virgin, Utah

Utah contains some of the most beautiful scenery in the United States. In April 1873 Hillers went back to the Zion Canyon area, or Mukuntuweap Canyon as Powell originally named it, where he prepared a series of photographs and stereographs on the Virgin River.

Hillers did some of his best work during that trip between 4 April and 22 May. While the stunning scenery lent itself to the task, Hillers had matured as a craftsman. Contemporary art historians have pointed out elements of the luminist tradition in Hillers' Virgin River photographs, a technique popular with nineteenth-century landscape painters and photographers.

PLATE 27

John Hillers
Nettle Creek, Utah

This photograph of Nettle Creek was taken in May or June of 1873 during Hillers' Utah expedition. This period was a high point in Hillers' career as a landscape photographer.

PLATE 28

John Hillers
The Three Patriarchs, Parunuweap Canyon, Virgin River Valley, Utah

These majestic buttes which border the Virgin River in southern Utah's Zion region were named the Three Patriarchs. Between each butte lies a young canyon in formation. Photographed in April 1873 by Hillers as part of his Virgin River Series, this image was taken just downstream from the Narrows in Parunuweap Canyon and the (now abandoned) settlement of Shunesburg, Utah. Parunuweap Canyon is located on the lower East Fork of the Virgin River.

Hillers spent four days wading through the icy waters of the Parunuweap Canyon Narrows. The Narrows denote a place on the river where the water reaches to the sheer canyon walls leaving no river bank. The canyon walls are high (2000 to 3000 feet/600 to 900 meters) and close together, usually too close to allow a boat to pass. However, the water is usually shallow enough to walk or wade through. Zion Canyon's massive, multicolored vertical cliffs and deep canyons were established as a national park in 1919.

PLATE 29

John Hillers
Pilling's Cascade

John Hillers photographed this lovely waterfall in Bullion Canyon in Utah, one of the many canyons explored by Hillers in May or June 1873.

PLATE 30

John Hillers
Virgin River Valley, Below Zion Canyon, Utah

The exquisite Virgin River Valley below the confluence of the north and east forks of the river was a sight to behold. In the lower left corner of the scene are the cultivated fields of the Mormon settlement of Virgin City. It was customary to obtain permission from community leaders before passing through Mormon lands, and the Powell Survey was no exception. Hillers exposed this and numerous other glass plate negatives in the Virgin River Valley between April and August 1873.

PLATE 31

Timothy O'Sullivan
Ruins in the Canyon de Chelly

This famous photograph of the ruins in the Canyon de Chelly was taken by O'Sullivan in 1873. The ruins are in a cavity in the rock wall that the canyon's ancient inhabitants reached by rope ladders or footholds carved into the rock.

PLATE 32

Timothy O'Sullivan
Canyon de Chelly

O'Sullivan took this overall view of the Canyon de Chelly which became a national monument in 1931, adding to the list of national treasures found in the state of Arizona. The few tents visible in the foreground belonged to the expedition.

PLATE 33

William Henry Jackson
*Front Range, Clear Creek and
Summit Counties*

William Henry Jackson was in Colorado in 1873 where he photographed a
number of views of the Front Range of
the Rocky Mountains. This view from
near Gray's Peak, the prominent feature
in this image, was later combined with
four other shots in a panorama of the
Front Range which included Clear
Creek, Summit, Grand, Boulder, and
Park Counties.

PLATE 34

William Henry Jackson
Hayden's Cathedral

While surveying with the Hayden expedition in the Uinta Mountains in
1873, Jackson photographed this mountain of purplish compact quartzite which
stood isolated in the middle of the valley
of Smith's Fork in Summit County,
Utah. It was estimated to rise 1500 feet
(500 meters) and resembled a Gothic
cathedral, which led members of the survey to christen it 'Hayden's Cathedral.'
The horizontal striations in the rock are
set in relief by the snow.

PLATE 35

Timothy O'Sullivan
The Head of Canyon de Chelly

In 1873 and 1875 Timothy O'Sullivan photographed the Southwest's canyons and pueblo ruins. The towering walls at the head of the Canyon de Chelly are the gateway to the now-famous White House ruins.

106. MOUNTAIN OF THE HOLY-CROSS

PLATE 36

William Henry Jackson
Mountain of the Holy Cross

The subject of legends for several decades, but never before confirmed, the Holy Cross was captured on film for the first time when Jackson photographed the site in 1873. The vertical arm of the cross is 1500 feet (500 meters) in length and 50 feet (15 meters) across. The horizonal arm varies with the seasons, but it averages 700 feet (210 meters) in length. The cross is a natural feature in the mountains of Eagle County, Colorado. The mountain is made of gneiss.

PLATE 37

William Henry Jackson
Topographical Work

Documenting the work done by members of the survey was part of Jackson's job as survey photographer for the years 1870-78 for the Hayden US Geological and Geographical Survey of the Territories. Here team members William Henry Holmes and GB Chittenden conduct topographical studies in 1874.

PLATE 38

William Henry Jackson
Rio Grande

Jackson took this picture from Wagon Wheel Gap of the columnar stratification of the basaltic bluffs bordering the Rio Grande in Mineral County, Colorado, in 1874.

THE RIO GRANDE, WAGON-WHEEL GAP. 123.

PLATE 39

John Hillers
Winslow Creek, Aquarius Plateau

This photograph was taken in southern Utah in July 1875. Winslow Creek was a tributary of the Escalante River, but it is no longer known by the name by which Hillers knew it. In 1965 the National Board of Geographic Names changed Winslow Creek to Pine Creek.

PLATE 40

William Henry Jackson
Rio Grande

This 1874 view of the Rio Grande between Lost Trail and Pole Creeks was taken by William Henry Jackson in Hinsdale County, Colorado. Jackson and many of his contemporaries followed the practice of setting long exposure times which resulted in photographs like this one with streaks in the sky made by the moving clouds and the surface of the water looking glassy.

PLATE 41

John Hillers
Unnamed Lake

Photographed by Hillers during his Utah trip in July 1875, this lake is located on the Aquarius Plateau in southern Utah.

PLATE 42

John Hillers
Canyon de Chelly

In 1879 or 1881, Hillers took this view of this starkly beautiful canyon in northeastern Arizona. Canyon de Chelly was home to the Anasazi people who flourished here from 700 AD to 1100 AD. They lived in apartment dwellings built into the cliffs and cultivated crops on the fertile banks of the river. The Anasazi disappeared suddenly when the climate of the region changed.

PLATE 43

John Hillers
Canyon de Chelly

This incredible canyon in north-eastern Arizona in the heart of Navajo country was photographed by Jack Hillers in 1879 or 1881 during one of his many trips through the Southwest as part of his duties as photographer for the Bureau of Ethnology. Canyon de Chelly provided Hillers with rich and interesting photographic opportunities. Canyon de Chelly became a national monument in 1931 and extends over an area of 83,840 acres (33,536 hectares).

PLATE 44

John Hillers
Captains of the Canyon

The 'captains' pictured in this photograph are also known as Spider Rock. They were photographed by Jack Hillers in 1879 or 1881 on one of his visits to Canyon de Chelly. Both William Henry Jackson and Timothy O'Sullivan photographed this ghostly village in the early 1870s.

NAVAJO CHURCH, NEAR FORT WINGATE

HILLERS

PLATE 45

John Hillers
Navajo Church

Hillers divided his time during the 1882 field season between Canyon de Chelly and Fort Wingate in western New Mexico.

Navajo Church, a rock formation near Fort Wingate, commands attention in this eerie landscape.

PLATE 46

John Hillers (?)
Yellowstone Falls

Attributed to John K Hillers, this photograph of Yellowstone Falls may have been taken as early as 1876, but more likely it was taken later. Hillers' work probably reached the widest audience of any nineteenth-century photographer, because he worked for government agencies in the business of disseminating information to the public. He also worked under the same person, John Wesley Powell, for 25 years and had a considerable amount of freedom in choosing his subjects.

PLATE 47

John Hillers
Detail of White House Ruin at Canyon de Chelly, Arizona

PLATE 48

John Hillers
White House Ruin at Canyon de Chelly

The White House is the centerpiece of the remarkable series of architectural wonders located in Canyon de Chelly. These apartment structures were constructed by the Anasazi, the ancestors of the Hopi and possibly other Pueblo groups, who flourished here between 700 AD and 1100 AD. On the canyon walls there is evidence of ancient and modern graffiti, the meaning of which is open to interpretation. Hillers took this photograph in 1879 or 1881 on one of his visits to the region.

PLATE 49

John Hillers
Cliff Dwellings

These ruins of cliff dwellings or gran-
aries in Walnut Canyon, Arizona, near
Flagstaff, were among the many that Jack
Hillers photographed in 1885. This canyon is now within Walnut Canyon National Monument. A gear box is visible
on the right. In the desert climate, the
natural process of decompostion is
slower. These structures, built by hand of
rock and mortar, have remained as
signposts of history.

PLATE 50

John Hillers
San Francisco Mountains

In 1885 during one of his several Arizona expeditions, Jack Hillers photographed these picturesque mountains
near Flagstaff named by the Spanish for
St Francis of Assisi. Note the initials
'EPH' carved in the tree, evidence that
the white man had ventured here.
According to the Hopi, sacred Ka-
china spirits live on the tops of these
mountains and travel north yearly to the
Hopi mesas to participate in the ceremonies in their honor.

PLATE 51

John Hillers
Road Into Yosemite Valley

This narrow wagon road was the only road into Yosemite Valley in 1892 when John Hillers went there to photograph the natural splendor. The ruts in the path were made by the wheels of mule-drawn wagons. Straight ahead is the stern but beautiful face of El Capitan. Beyond the mountains, the regal Half Dome directs its stunning profile north.

PLATE 52

John Hillers
Yosemite Valley

Yosemite Valley is a place teaming with wildlife, although much less today than in 1892 when John Hillers took this view of El Capitan from the banks of the Merced River in the valley floor. Yosemite is home to many species of fish, deer, black bear, birds, otters, the giant sequoia redwood, ponderosa pine, cedar, Douglas fir and a staggering assortment of wild flowers, whose annual display makes the High Sierra meadows even more gorgeous.

PLATE 53

John Hillers
Merced River in Yosemite Valley

The Merced River meanders through Yosemite Valley. When alpine glaciers moved through the canyon of the Merced River, the ice carved through weaker sections of granite, plucking and scouring rock but leaving harder, more solid portions—such as El Capitan and Cathedral Rocks—intact. John Hillers captured this beautiful reflection of El Capitan in the calm waters of the Merced.

PLATE 54

John Hillers
Yosemite, Home of the Storm Gods

Like Hillers, who was drawn to Yosemite Valley over a hundred years ago, people still come here to revel in the land's incomparable beauty. While the landscape is formidable, for many visitors to the park it is the quality of light which transfixes and suspends the moment, making each person wish that they could capture on film how it felt to be there.

PLATE 55

John Hillers
Yosemite Valley

John Hillers explored the Yosemite Valley in 1892. Between field work for the Bureau of Ethnology and the Geological Survey, Hillers assembled thousands of prints documenting the land and people of the United States. His photographs of Yosemite Valley certainly do justice to this beautiful national park, established just two years prior to this photograph.

PLATE 56

John Hillers
View Down Yosemite Valley

In this Hillers photograph of Yosemite Valley, the lush vegetation lining the Merced River contrasts with the stark granite of El Capitan.

Plate 57

John Hillers
Merced River

It is evident by the number of images John Hillers made of Yosemite Valley that he was captivated by the enchanted landscape. His photos convey the majesty of the area, and the restorative power of the light.

Plate 58

John Hillers
Big Trees in Mariposa Grove

Mariposa Grove is the largest of three sequoia groves in California's Yosemite National Park. It is home to the Grizzly Giant, a 2700-year-old tree considered to be the oldest of all sequoias.

PLATE 59

D Griffiths
Canyon de Chelly

Canyon de Chelly and its splendid Anasazi ruins had been the object of several photographic and ethnographic expeditions (see Plates 39-42 and 44) by the time that D Griffiths arrived in 1903 to record these disassembled wagons.

Neil M Judd
West of Navajo Mountain

Neil M Judd photographed this pack
train west of Navajo Mountain on the
way to Rainbow Bridge in Utah in 1909.

PLATE 61

JE Stimson
Gannett Peak, Dinwoody Creek

JE Stimson of Cheyenne, Wyoming, worked as a photographer from the late 1890s until 1942. His life's work consists of over 7520 images and glass plate negatives. This breathtaking vista is an example of the unspoiled Mountain West. Gannett Peak is in the Wind River Range, south of Yellowstone National Park.

PLATE 62

JE Stimson
Wind River Range

Taken from the Dinwoody Valley looking into Wyoming's Wind River Range, JE Stimson captured the rugged beauty of the region.

PLATE 63

JE Stimson
Sublett Mountain

Stimson took this photo of Sublett Mountain, west of the Continental Divide in Idaho early in the twentieth century when the region was still unspoiled.

PLATE 64

JE Stimson
Tetons from the Gros Ventre Side

The Teton Range is one of the most spectacular mountain ranges in the United States. It is located on the western edge of Wyoming, and seen here from the Gros Ventre side. The youngest of the mountains in the Rocky Mountain system, the Teton Range displays some of North America's oldest rocks. The tallest peak is Grand Teton, which rises to 13,766 feet (4130 meters) above sea level.

PLATE 65

JE Stimson
Sublett Peak and Upper Lake

One of the most important photographers working in the Yellowstone and Snake River country at the turn of the twentieth century, JE Stimson took many expressive photographs, including this view of Sublett Peak from Upper Lake.

PLATE 66

JE Stimson
Mateo Tepee or Devil's Tower

Mateo Tepee or Devil's Tower is an unusual geologic feature that has inspired many legends for Native Americans as well as white newcomers. Located in eastern Wyoming, it rises to an elevation of 5112 feet (1534 meters). Stimson photographed Devil's Tower around the time that it was dedicated as a national monument in 1906. The river in the foreground is the Belle Fourche which means 'beautiful fork.'

PLATE 67

JE Stimson
Hell's Half Acre

Named for its resemblence to the hot, dry and barren place that Hell is supposed to be, Hell's Half Acre provided Stimson with interesting photo opportunities.

86

PLATE 68

JE Stimson
Gargoyle

This close-up of one of the rock formations in Hell's Half Acre, aptly called
a gargoyle, is a reminder that beauty is in
the eye of the beholder.

PLATE 69

Edgar Lowell Steele
Wild Mustangs

Edgar Lowell Steele photographed many scenes like this in northern Arizona. Only one of the wild mustangs in this 1928 photo seems to be aware of the photographer.

Plate 70

Edgar Lowell Steele
Mustang Mare and Colts

Edgar Lowell Steele photographed this mustang mare and colts in northwestern Arizona in 1928. The wild horse is an enduring symbol of the unspoiled West in American mythology.

PLATE 71

Edgar Lowell Steele
Monument Valley

Arizona offers panoramic vistas of
sunrises and sunsets against the rugged
cliffs such as the one shown in this photograph. Steele took this photograph in
Monument Valley, a magical place on
the border between Arizona and Utah,
in 1932.

PLATE 72

Edgar Lowell Steele
Three Fingers of the Gods

This desert landscape was taken at Monument Valley, Arizona, on 1 October 1932. The strange and beautiful rock formations in Monument Valley have been named and renamed by visitors who imagined fanciful shapes and creatures in these stunning stone monoliths.

PLATE 73

Edgar Lowell Steele
Monument Valley

This view taken by Edgar Steele on 1 October 1932 captured the majesty of the single monument rising out of the earth under a cloudless sky.

PLATE 74

Edgar Lowell Steele
Monument Valley

This is one of two such mountains in Monument Valley known as 'The Mitten.' Steele took this view in 1932 when he traveled throughout Arizona and New Mexico on a photography excursion. Today, Monument Valley is one of the most photographed areas in the Southwest. It has appeared as the set for countless advertisements and television commercials.

PLATE 75

George Alexander Grant
Cape Sebastian Viewed From the North

This region's rugged, isolated nature does not detract from its beauty. As Grant has shown in this moody image of Cape Sebastian, the Oregon Coast is a place where nature's harmony reigns supreme. This photo was taken in 1938.

PLATE 76

George Alexander Grant
Cape Sebastian Viewed From the South

This second view of Cape Sebastian taken by Grant in 1938 shows the Cape from a point just north of the mouth of the Pistol River. The rugged Oregon coastline is peppered with boulders lying half-submerged in the surf. To be present when one of these megaliths falls would be an exciting event.

Karl Birdsall
*Adobe Walls At An Old Spanish
Mission Church*

   The Rio Grande Valley of New Mexico has some beautiful adobe buildings
like this mission church photographed
by Karl Birdsall in 1939. John K Hillers
also spent many months between 1879
and 1882 in this area photographing the
Rio Grande pueblos.

PLATE 78

Karl Birdsall
Old Spanish Mission Church

   Birdsall photographed this church in
1939. It is set in the Rio Grande Valley of
New Mexico, an area of open expanses of
cactus and scrub brush puncutated by
rugged mountains. This mission was still
in use at the time.

PLATE 79

PLATE 80

Ansel Adams
Clouds, White Pass

Ansel Adams
Near Death Valley

Through the use of colored filters and darkroom developing techniques, Ansel Adams produced images of exquisite beauty which forever affected the way people perceived nature.

Death Valley National Monument in California, lies between the Panamint Range and the Amargosa Range close to the Nevada border. The area was made a national monument in 1933. Badwater in Death Valley is the lowest point in the United States with an altitude of 282 feet (85 meters) below sea level. Ansel Adams was drawn to the wild and desolate places.

PLATE 81

Ansel Adams
Bishop Pass

Bishop, California, on the Owens River in the eastern Sierra, is a point on the way to many national park and national monument destinations in California including Yosemite, Kings Canyon, Sequoia, Death Valley and Devil's Postpile.

PLATE 82

Ansel Adams
Owens Valley from Sawmill Pass

Owens Valley in California's eastern Sierra foothills, was photographed by Ansel Adams on one of his many travels across the western United States. Sparse vegetation and sapphire lakes color the rugged mountain range.

PLATE 83

Ansel Adams
Middle Fork at Kings River

The Sierra Nevada were a favorite photo subject for Ansel Adams, who made his home at Yosemite for many years in the early twentieth century. The combination of terrain, light and air quality invigorated his perceptions of nature and man's place in it, leading Adams to make exquisite portraits like this one.

PLATE 84

Ansel Adams
North Dome, Kings River Canyon

The North Dome in Kings River Canyon has an imposing granite face chiseled by ancient glaciers. Kings Canyon was established as a national park in 1940 and is administered jointly with Sequoia National Park, established in 1890. It is here on the western slope of the Sierra that the the giant sequoia grows. The naturalist John Muir was the first to call the Sierra 'the Range of Light,' a name that photographers would bring to life during the next century.

PLATE 85

Ansel Adams
Grand Canyon National Park

The series of photographs Adams took of the Grand Canyon of the Colorado, captured the majesty of the landscape like no other photographer before him.

PLATE 86

Ansel Adams
Grand Canyon National Park

In this characteristically Adams photograph of a Grand Canyon panorama the dark shadows take on a mysterious quality that give the canyon's peaks the appearance of floating islands.

PLATE 87

Ansel Adams
Grand Canyon National Park

Adams directs the eye to the rock formation in the foreground. The solitary
sentinel gazes into the hazy canyon as
layer upon layer of rock waits for the sun.

PLATE 88

Ansel Adams
Grand Canyon National Park

From below the rim, Ansel Adams
photographed the sun spilling into the
canyon and a sliver of the mighty Colorado River.

PLATE 89

Ansel Adams
Canyon de Chelly

This amazing panorama of the river valley in Canyon de Chelly, Arizona, is one of the more evocative views taken of this ancient land. Adams succeeded in representing 'the most enduring' and massive aspects of the world.'

PLATE 90

Ansel Adams
Zion National Park

Adams went to Zion National Park in 1941, a wild, rugged country of plateaus and canyons in southern Utah. With its multicolored sandstone cliffs Zion deserves its name as 'the heavenly city of God.'

PLATE 91

Ansel Adams
Old Faithful Geyser

The eruption of Old Faithful at Yellowstone National Park was a sight to behold, and Ansel Adams captured the geyser's performance perfectly. As the photographer for the Sierra Club and a one-man publicity firm for the wilderness, it was photos like this one that made the public aware of the incredible natural wonders that were worthy of preserving for posterity.

PLATE 92

Ansel Adams
The Fishing Cone, Yellowstone Lake

The Yellowstone National Park is home to 11 species of fish, and offers fishing permits. Ansel Adams found this fishing cone in Yellowstone Lake to be a fine spot to drop a line.

PLATE 93

Ansel Adams
Roaring Mountain

The steam rises from Roaring Mountain in the background. In the foreground, a stand of dead trees gives this view an eerie quality. Ansel Adams visited Yellowstone National Park in 1942.

PLATE 94

Ansel Adams
Jupiter Terrace, Fountain Geyser Pool

Jupiter Terrace is one of the spectacular terraces of travertine (calcium carbonate) deposited daily by the mineral rich water in Yellowstone.

PLATE 95

Ansel Adams
In Rocky Mountain National Park

The lush valley and snow-covered peaks of Rocky Mountain National Park in Colorado are destined to remain part of the unspoiled West.

PLATE 96

Ansel Adams
In Rocky Mountain National Park

One third of Rocky Mountain National Park is above treeline, where tundra predominates as seen in this view. A harsh fragile environment, the alpine tundra shares many plants and animals with the Arctic. This spectacular park was established in 1915.

PLATE 97

Ansel Adams
In Rocky Mountain National Park

At the lower elevations in Rocky
Mountain National Park, the slopes are
wooded with evergreen forests and
dotted with sparkling lakes.

PLATE 98

Ansel Adams
*Moraine, Rocky Mountain National
Park*

Ansel Adams chose to print relatively
few subjects from his western series.
These rocks resemble the weather-
beaten blocks of the pyramids in Egypt.

PLATE 99

Ansel Adams
In Glacier National Park

Partially obscured by clouds, the dark mountains in Glacier National Park are home to the grizzly bear and bighorn sheep, two formidable examples of independent personalities born in the unspoiled West.

PLATE 100

Ansel Adams
In Glacier National Park

The awesome peaks of Glacier National Park in Montana inspire visitors to the park as they did Ansel Adams, as evidenced by this high-contrast image. His use of red and orange filters helped to darken the sky and display clouds much more dramatically.

PLATE 101

PLATE 102

Ansel Adams
Tetons from Signal Mountain

The Teton Range, photographed from Signal Mountain (7593 feet/2728 meters) overlooking Jackson Hole, a valley that runs the length of the Grand Teton National Park.

Ansel Adams
The Tetons—Snake River

This view taken in Grand Teton National Park gives credence to the name of this river—the Snake. Its serpentine path flows through Jackson Hole, Wyoming, contributing to making this park one of the most scenic in the system.

PLATE 103

PLATE 104

Ansel Adams
Two Medicine Lake,
Glacier National Park

Ansel Adams
Evening at Lake McDonald

Sinopah Mountain looms over Two Medicine Lake, named for the joint medicine lodge ceremonies that were to be held by the Blackfeet and Blood. Adams' photographic treatment of this sacred place conveys the presence of powerful spiritual forces that dwell here.

Adams used the soft light of the evening to capture the peaceful mood in this photo looking south across Lake McDonald on the west side of Glacier National Park, Montana.

PLATE 105

Karl Birdsall
*Close-up of Ruins at Mesa Verde
National Monument, Colorado*

Mesa Verde National Park preserves a
spectacular remnant of the Anasazi culture, a prehistoric people who inhabited
this canyon in Colorado from 700 AD to
1100 AD. After their disappearance,
their descendants, the Puebloans, moved
in. The buildings were handmade from
sandstone shaped into blocks and held in
place by mortar made of mud and river
water. Karl Birdsall photographed this
scene in 1942 shortly before his death.

PLATE 106

Bradford Washburn
*Camp at Southeast Foot of Mount
Bertha, Alaska*

The tents of this base camp are
dwarfed by the majestic sweep of the
peaks behind them. The national park
system in Alaska now contains more
than 51 million acres (20 million hectares), or 13 percent of the state's 375
million acres (150 million hectares).
Bradford Washburn took this photograph in 1940. To keep the integrity of
the whites of the snow and the clouds,
Washburn, like Ansel Adams, employed
colored filters.

INDEX

Adams, Ansel 4, 5, 18-19, 98-123, 125, 127
Alaska 18, 19, *125*
Amargosa Range 98
Anasazi Indians 16, 124
Apache Indians 10
Appleton's Journal of Literature 10, 11
Appomattox, Virginia 12
Aquarius Plateau, Utah *19, 56-57*
Arctic 114
Arizona 4, 10, 11, 16, 17, 18, 19, *32*, 42, *45, 46, 50-51, 60-63, 66-69, 78, 88-93, 108*
Arkansas River 54
Artist Point, Yellowstone National Park 26
Badwater, Death Valley National Monmument 98
Beaman, EO 15, 17
Belle Fourche River, Wyoming *85*
Birdsall, Karl 96, 97, 124
Bishop Pass, California *100*
Blackfeet 122
Black Sand Spring, Yellowstone National Park 25
Blood 122
Blue Creek, Utah 12
Boston, Massachusetts 10, 11
Boulder County, Colorado 52
Brady, Mathew 8
Bullion Canyon, Utah *40*
Bull Run, Battle of 8
California 8, 10, 17, 18, *20-25*, 42, *70-77, 98-103*
California, Gulf of 42
Calumet cameras 126
Campbell, CR *16*
Canada 18, 19
Canonita 18
Canyon de Chelly, Arizona 19, *50-51, 54, 60-61, 62, 66, 108*
Cape Sebastian, Oregon *94, 95*
Captains of the Canyon, Arizona *see* Spider Rock, Arizona
Carlsbad Caverns National Park 19
Carnegiea gigantea see Saguaro cactus
Carson Desert, Nevada *31*
Castle Geyser, Yellowstone National Park *24*
Castle Rocks, Utah 13
Cataract Canyon, Utah 42
Cathedral Rocks, Yosemite National Park 72
Central Pacific Railroad 10, 11, 12
Cheyenne, Wyoming 14
Chicago, Illinois 11
Chittenden, GB *56*
Church of Jesus Christ of Latter-day Saints 50
Civil War (1861-1865) 8, 10, 12, 13, 17, *32*
Clear Creek, Colorado 16, *54*
Clear Creek County, Colorado 52
Cliff dwellings 68

Colorado 8, 14, 16, 17, 18, 19, 42, 52, *57, 58*, 114, *124*
Colorado River 4, 10, 17, *22, 34, 38*, 42, *43, 107*
Colorado River Canyon, Arizona 53
Colorado Territory 13
Colter, John 14
Columnar basalt *39, 56*
Corinne, Utah 12
Crimean War (1855) 8
Cunningham Gulch, Colorado Territory 13
Curtis, Edward S 18
Daguerre, Louis Jacques 8
Daguerreotypes 8
Dana Butte, Utah *44*
Darkrooms, portable *9,* 10, 12, 14, 16
Death Rock, Utah 13
Death Valley, California 10, *98-99*
Death Valley National Monument 10, *98-99*, 100
Dellenbaugh, FS *18, 44*
Denver, Colorado 16, 17
Detroit, Michigan 17
Devil's Anvil, Arizona *34*
Devil's Postpile National Monument 100
Devil's Slide, Utah 13
Devil's Tower, Wyoming *see* Mateo Tepee, Wyoming
Dinwoody Creek, Wyoming *80*
Dinwoody Valley, Wyoming *81*
Dirty Devil River, Utah *18*
Douglas County, Colorado 8
Dry plates 10, 17, 18
Dry films 16
Eagle County, Colorado 55
East Fork River 11
Eastman, George 10, 18
El Capitan, Yosemite National Park *70, 71,* 72, *75*
England 16
Escalante River 58
Evil Merodach *10*
Explorer's Column *see* Spider Rock, Arizona
Fennemore, James 17, 38, 39
The Fishing Cone, Yellowstone National Park *111*
Fort Bridger, Wyoming 14
Fort Wingate, New Mexico 64
Fountain Geyser Pool, Yellowstone National Park *113*
France 8
Fremont, General John 8
Fremont Expedition (1842) 8
Fremont Peak, Wyoming 17
Front Range, Rocky Mountains *52*
Gannett Peak, Wyoming *80*
Gardner, James T 16
Geyser Basin, Yellowstone National Park *35*
Gilbert, Grove Karl 18
Glacier Bay, Alaska 19
Glacier National Park 19, *118, 119, 122-123*
Glen Canyon, Utah 42
Golden Spike Ceremony, Promontory, Utah 13

Grand Canyon *2*, 10, 17, 19, 34, *38, 39*, 42, 44, *59*
  North Rim 38
Grand Canyon National Park *104, 105, 106, 107*
Grand Canyon of the Yellowstone, Yellowstone National Park 15, *38, 127*
Grand County, Colorado 52
Grand Teton National Park 19, *33, 120, 121, 126*
Granite Canyon, Arizona 45
Granite Rapids, Grand Canyon *44*
Grant, George Alexander 5, 94, 95
Grant, President Ulysses S 15
Gray's Peak, Rocky Mountain National Park 52
Great Basin 10
Great Salt Lake, Utah 10
Green River 15, 17, *30*
Greer, Mary 12
Griffiths, D 78
Gros Ventre Range 82
Grotto Geyser Cone, Yellowstone National Park *65*
Half Dome, Yosemite National Park 19
Hanging Rock, Utah 13
Harper's New Monthly Magazine 28
Hayden, Dr Ferdinand Vanderveer 10, *11,* 13-17
Hayden's Cathedral *53*
Hayden Expeditions 8, *11,* 12, 14-17, 18, 26, 33-39, 52-53, 56-58
  (1870) 14
  (1871) *11,* 14-15, 26, 30, 36, 37
  (1872) 16, 33-35, 38, 39
  (1873) 16, 52, 53
  (1874) 8, 16, 56-58
  (1875) 13, 16
  (1877) 16-17
  (1878) 17
Haynes, F Jay 65
Hell's Half Acre, Wyoming *86, 87*
Hillers, John Karl 'Jack' 15, *17,* 17-18, *18, 19,* 30, *38, 39-49, 56-64, 66-77*
Hinsdale County, Colorado *58*
Holmes, William Henry *56*
Hoover Dam, Nevada 42
Hopi pueblos 17
Ickes, Harold 19
Idaho 10, *20, 21, 23,* 82, 84
Illinois 11, 17
Illinois Normal University 17
Indians *see* Native Americans
Indian Territory 18
Inuit Indians 18
Jackson, Ed 11
Jackson, Mary (Greer) 12, 14
Jackson, William Henry 8, 10-17, 18, 19, *24-30,* 33, 35-37, 52, 53, 55, 56-58 126, 127
Jackson Brothers 11
Jackson Hole, Wyoming *120, 121*
Johnson, WD, Jr *18*
Judd, Neil M 79

Jupiter Terrace, Yellowstone National Park *113*
Kanab, Utah 15
Kanab Canyon, Utah 44, *45, 46*
King, Clarence 8, 10, 17, 18
King Expedition (1867-1868) 8, 10, 18, 26, 28, 29, 30
King Solomon Mountain, Colorado Territory *13*
Kings Canyon National Park 100, 102, *103*
Kings River *102*
Kings River Canyon *103*
Kodak Brownie cameras 18
Korona cameras 19
Ladore Canyon, Utah *30*
Lake McDonald, Glacier National Park *122*
Lake Mead, Nevada 42
Lake Powell, Utah 42
Langford, NP 14
Lava Falls Rapids, Grand Canyon *39*
Lewis and Clark Expedition (1804-1806) 14
Lincoln, President Abraham 8
Lincoln County, Wyoming 16, 33
Little Firehole Falls, Yellowstone National Park *30*
London, England 16
Longs Peak, Colorado 16, *128*
Loring, Frederick W 10, *10*
Lost Trail Creek, Colorado 58
McAlpin, David 5
McKee, Thomas 18
Mammoth Hot Springs, Yellowstone National Park 14, *33*
Manassass, Battle of 8
Mancos Canyon, Colorado 16
Man-Who-Picks-Up-Stones-Running *see* Hayden, Dr Ferdinand Vanderveer
Marble Canyon, Arizona 42, *43*
Marble Pinnacle, Arizona *46*
Mariposa Grove, Yosemite National Park *77*
Massachusetts 10
Mateo Tepee, Wyoming *85*
Merced River *71, 72, 76*
Mesa Verde, Colorado 16, 18
Mesa Verde National Monument *124*
Mexico 4, 42
Michigan 17
Mineral County, Colorado *57*
Minnetaree Indians 38
Mississippi River 11
Missouri 11
Missouri River 38
'The Mitten,' Arizona *93*
Montana 10, 17, 18, 19, 118
Montrose, Colorado 18
Monument Rock, Utah 13
Monument Valley, Arizona 19, *88-93*
Moqui pueblos 16
Moraines 54, *117*
Mormons *see* Church of Jesus Christ of Latter-day Saints
Morse, Samuel FB 8

Mountain of the Holy Cross, Colorado 55
Mt Bertha, Alaska *125*
Mt Hayden *see* Grand Teton National Park
Mt McKinley, Alaska 19
Mt Rainier, Washington 19
Mt Sheridan, Wyoming *7*
Muir, John 102
Mukuntuweap Canyon, Utah *see* Zion Canyon, Utah
Mukuntuweap Valley, Utah *17*
Mural Project 4, 108
Mustangs *4, 88*
Muybridge, Eadweard 19
Nankoweap Canyon, Arizona *43*
National Board of Geographic Names 58
National monuments *1, 124*
National parks *7*, 10, *11*, 14, 15, 18, 19, *33-39*, 48, *59*, *70-77, 104, 105, 106, 107, 109-119, 122, 125, 126, 127*
National Park Service 4, 5
Native Americans 10, 11, 13, 16, 17, 18, 38, 62, 66, 96, 124
Navajo Church, New Mexico *64*
Navajo Mountain, Utah *79*
Nebraska 11, 13
Needle Rocks, Utah 13
Nettle Creek, Utah *48*
Nevada 10, 11, *31*, 42, 52, 98
New Mexico 16, 17, 18, 19, 42, 52, *64*, 66, *96, 97*
New York 8, 10, 28
New York City, New York 8, 19
Niagara Falls, New York 28, 27
Niepce, Joseph Nicephore 8
North Dome, California *103*
Nowell, Frank 18
Oak Grove, Arizona *32*
Oberlin College, Ohio 13
Ogden, Utah 12
Ohio 12, 13
Oklahoma Territory 18
Old Faithful, Yellowstone National Park *34, 35*, 110
Olympic Peninsula, Washington 19
Omaha, Nebraska 11, 13
Opuntia see Prickly Pear Cactus
Oregon 5, *94, 95*
Oregon-Mormon Trail 14, 30
O'Sullivan, Timothy 8, 10, 11, 18, 20-23, 31, 34, 50, 51, 54
Overland Trail 14
Owens River 100
Owens Valley, California *101*
Pacific Ocean *5*, 11, 18, 19
Panama, Isthmus of 10
Panamint Range 98
Paria Creek, Utah *22*
Paris, France 8
Park County, Colorado 52
Parunuweap Canyon, Utah *49*
    The Narrows 48

Parunuweap River 17
Peabody, Henry 17
Pennsylvania 18
Philadelphia, Pennsylvania 18
Pikes Peak, Colorado 14
Pilling's Cascade, Utah *50*
Pine Creek, Utah *see* Winslow Creek, Utah
Pistol River, Oregon 95
Platte Canyon, Colorado *9*
Pole Creek, Colorado 58
Powell, Clem 17
Powell, Major John Wesley 10, 15, 17-18, 47, 127
Powell Expeditions *15*, 17-18, 38-49, 56-63
    (1871) 17
    (1872) 17, *18*, 38-44
    (1873) 17, 47-51
    (1875) 18, 56-58
    (1876) 59
    (1879) 60-63
Prickly Pear Cactus *45*
Promontory, Utah 10, 12, 13
Prospect Mountain 16
Pueblo of Tewa 16
Puebloans 124
Pulpit Rock, Utah 13
The Pyramids, Egypt 116
'Range of Light' *see* Sierra Nevada
Reflected Tower, Utah *47*
Rio Grande *57, 58*
Rio Grande Valley 18, 19, *96, 97*
Rio Virgin *see* Virgin River
Roaring Mountain, Yellowstone National Park *112*
Rochester, New York 10
Rocky Mountain National Park 19, *114, 115, 116, 117, 128*
Rocky Mountains 10, 16, 19, *52*
Saguaro cactus *1*
Saguaro National Monument *1*
Salt Lake City, Utah 8, 10, 13, 17
Sampson, John 28
San Francisco, California 8, 10, 18, 68
San Francisco Mountains *69*
San Juan County, Colorado Territory 13
San Juan River 52
Santa Fe, New Mexico 16, 19
Sawmill Pass, California *101*
Schicrenbeck, Elizabeth 18
Scovill cameras 16
Sequoia National Park 100, 102
Sequoia redwood trees *77*
Shiloh, Battle of 17
Shoshone Canyon, Idaho 20, *21*, 23
Shoshone Falls, Idaho 20, *21, 23*
Shunesburg, Utah *48*
Sierra Blanca Range *32*
Sierra Club 18, 110
Sierra Nevada 10, 23, 28, 100, 102

Signal Mountain, Wyoming 120
Sinopah Mountain, Montana *122*
Smith's Fork, Utah 53
Smithsonian Institution, Washington, DC 18
    Bureau of Ethnology 18
Snake River *26, 27, 29, 121*
Spanish Mission Churches *96, 97*
Spider Rock, Arizona *52, 63*
Steele, Edgar Lowell 4, 89
Stereoscopic cameras 14, 16, 18, 52
Stimson, JE 80-87
St Louis, Missouri 11
Sublett Mountain, Idaho *82, 84*
Summit County, Colorado 52
Summit County, Utah 53
Teton Basin 16
Teton Range 15, 16, *16, 33 83, 120, 121*
Teton River 16
Thompson, Almon Harris *14*, 18
Three Fingers of the Gods, Arizona *89*
The Three Patriarchs, Utah *49*
Tlingit Indians 18
Tower Creek, Wyoming 14
Tower Creek Falls, Yellowstone National Park *36, 37*
Transcontinental railroad 10, 12
Two Medicine Lake, Glacier National Park *122*
Uintah, Utah 12
Uinta Mountains 14, 53
Union Army 13, 17
Union Pacific Railroad 10, 11, 12, 13
University of Pennsylvania 10, 13
Upper Firehole, Yellowstone National Park *24*
Upper Lake, Idaho *84*
US Army 10
US Centennial Exposition 18
US Congress 12, 14, 15, 17
US Department of the Interior 19
US Geological Exploration of the Fortieth Parallel *see* King Expedition
US Geological & Geographical Survey of the Territories 10, *11*
    Division One 10, 18
    Division Two 10, 15, 17, 18
US Geologic Survey 10, 18
US Geographical Survey 18
US War Department 8, 10
US War Department Survey *see* Wheeler Expedition
Utah 8, 10, 12, 13, 15, 17, 18, *30*, 42, *44, 45*, 47-51, *56-57, 58, 79*
Ute Indians 18
Vermont 10, 11
Virginia 12
Virgin City, Utah *50*
Virgin River 17, *47, 49, 51*
Wagon Wheel Gap, Colorado 57
Walnut Canyon, Arizona 68
L Wamerke 16

Warren, Ohio 12
Wasatch Mountains 12, 23
Washburn, Bradford 125
Washburn, Henry D 14
Washee Mountains 23
Washington 19
Washington, DC 14, 16, 18, 19
West Point 10
Wheeler, Captain George Montague 10, 11, 17, 52
Wheeler Expeditions 10, 11, 18, 30, 52
    (1871) 10, 31
    (1873) 52, 53
    (1875) 10, 52
Wet plates 10, 12, 19
White House Ruin, Arizona 54, *66*
White Mountains 52
Wild horses *see* Mustangs
Willard lenses 13
Wind River Mountains 17, *81*
Winslow Creek, Utah 58
Wratten 29 red filter 19
Wyoming *7*, 10, 13, 14, 16, 17, 19, *39, 80, 81, 83, 85-87*, 120
Wyoming Territory 11, 15
Yellowstone Falls, Yellowstone National Park 15, *26, 27, 29, 59, 127*
Yellowstone Lake, Yellowstone National Park *7, 110*
Yellowstone National Park *7*, 10, *11*, 14, 15, 19, *24-30, 59, 65, 110-113, 127*
Yellowstone River 11, 14, *39, 59*
Yosemite National Park 18, 19, *70-77*
Yosemite Valley, Yosemite National Park 18, 19, *70-77*, 100
Yukon Territory 18
Zion Canyon, Utah 17, *47, 50*
Zion National Park 17, 19, 48, *109*
Zuni Indians 66
Zuni Mountains 52

PLATE 107

Ansel Adams
Longs Peak, Rocky Mountain National Park

Overleaf: Longs Peak is the highest peak in Rocky Mountain National Park, cresting at 14,255 feet (4350 meters). In the 1940s Ansel Adams achieved this breathtaking panorama of the rugged area explored by John Wesley Powell in 1868.